True, this book is a delight to read—but please don't let the good humor, the deft turns of phrase, the endearing bemusement, and obvious likeability of the author fool you: *Green Card* is an acutely serious contribution to the literature of immigration in our times. Áine Greaney's deeply interior vignettes also look outward, asking us to rethink something at the heart of the American experience, the psychic and societal consequences of being an American–in-process in a nation that is itself in process.

 —James Silas Rogers, author, *Irish-American Autobiography* and editor, *New Hibernia Review*

Áine Greaney's deft, subtle, and deceptively quiet essays lead from the every day incident to the heart-breaking but never sentimental examination of the nexus of identity and "home." She dexterously shows the immigrant glancing back to her past even as she looks to the uncertainties of the present and hope of acceptance. In this collection, the reader can also find that the foreign becomes warmly familiar.

 —Sandra Hunter, author, *Trip Wires*

GREEN CARD & OTHER ESSAYS

GREEN CARD & OTHER ESSAYS

ÁINE GREANEY

Wising Up Press Collective
Wising Up Press

Wising Up Press
P.O. Box 2122
Decatur, GA 30031-2122
www.universaltable.org

Catalogue-in-Publication data is on file with the Library of Congress.
LCCN: 2019901369

Wising Up ISBN: 978-1-7324514-2-1

TABLE OF CONTENTS

It made me think of the borders we all cross, the distances we've all come from what feels like home. Who lives at home, in America, now?

Sue Miller, *The World Below*

INTRODUCTION

Once, at age nineteen, I took the train across the Irish countryside to start my final (senior) year at my Dublin college. A month before, in late August, my live-in grandmother had died of pancreatic cancer. After the wake was over and our extended family had all departed our tiny country village, we kids didn't know how to talk about the grief or loss or what that empty armchair next to the living room range actually meant. So from illness to death to bereavement, it had been a tough summer.

As my train juddered between small-town stations, I couldn't wait to re-join my college clique and all our giggly undergrads' chatter. I pushed down my grief to muster up an urbane and urban version of myself that, the previous spring, I had left behind on that red brick, leafy campus on the south side of our capital city.

Earlier that summer, my college best friend had written (this was way, way pre-cell phones) to say that she was returning to college a week before the start of term. There, she would secure a cheap, month-to-month flat where she and our other friends would bunk in and camp out while we scanned the daily classifieds and fanned out across the college-adjacent neighborhoods to find a large, share-able apartment or house.

From the Dublin station, I took two city buses to the apartment of a family friend—an older woman who had agreed to let me stay a few nights while I connected up with my friends and we launched our search. At that older woman's attic flat, I deposited my bags to head back across the city to see my pals.

We squealed. We hugged. We caught up on summer news. Then, the room fell silent as the girls sat, tribunal-style, on the twin beds. They needed to tell me something. Yes, they were going to find a shared student rental. But I was not invited. They had discussed it and I was just not roommate material.

To my horror, I heard myself pushing past the lump in my throat to plead and ask: "But . . . but . . . why?"

They fidgeted. They looked at their feet.

I was untidy and messy. Sometimes, I ate too much from my best friend's care packages from her mother. I asked to borrow their clothes. And, worst of all, I often had bouts of silent melancholy.

Then, one girl summarized their plight and closed the conversation: "Look, Áine. You're . . . well, you're just not *like* us."

I knew, of course, what they meant. They were from middle-class families. Their fathers were civil servants or business owners. Their mothers mailed them homemade cookies and cakes and packets of new underwear. They didn't wear hand-me-down jeans. And, although they all hailed from provincial small towns, their speech wasn't quite as dotted with Irish, which is to say as country-sounding, as mine.

For two years, I had felt it, heard it, suspected it. But now I knew: On campus, at least among my chosen college clique, I was "other."

I pounded down the apartment house stairs. Instead of catching a bus, I walked down through Rathmines, then across the canal bridge and all the way down the South Circular Road. On the way, at the bus stops and on the footpaths, I avoided people's eyes while urging myself *for the love of Christ* to stop sobbing, to get it together before I got to that older woman's attic flat. However, as with all of our gut-spilling sorrows, there was no stopping and no separating all the old griefs from this new one. There was no dividing line between family bereavement and youthful ostracization.

As it turned out, that older woman let me stay on and share the rent in that flat and neighborhood where I stayed for the entire college year. She was often at work or out of town, so I was often alone. I came to adore that gritty, Dublin neighborhood where most of the men seemed to work for the Guinness Brewery and the women seemed to work at the Players Wills cigarette factory. Each outfit gave their workers an employee benefit of three free pints per day (Guinness) and discounted cartons of cigarettes (Players Wills). So out my kitchen window, I watched these workers—some obviously married couples—as they stood at the city bus stop cradling their day's goodies. On Saturday mornings I joined my neighbors to haggle and chat over the stalls of fruit and potatoes and chicken legs in the nearby street market. Overall, I recall that year as the best of my young life, when all that city-bound solitude seemed like a homecoming to my real and better self.

Why do I tell this story now, thirty-seven years later, and as part of a book on being an immigrant in America? I'm not sure, except to say that this was my first big brush with being an outsider, with "otherness."

Back then, Ireland was almost 100% ethnically and religiously homogenous. Like many post-colonial nations, we had replaced the colonizer-versus-native divide with our own, homegrown social-class system. And yes, this class system was perpetuated by the Catholic church that, in turn, had no formal separation from our government, healthcare or education.

That night in Dublin, I wasn't mature enough to know that this "othering" business is a form of voluntary and willful blindness. By not looking beyond appearances, we eclipse everything else about that other person. Even now, it shocks me that I had spent two years with a group of college girls and, despite all those late-night dormitory chats, despite all our treks across the city to concerts and pubs and raucous house parties, we had revealed little or nothing of our real selves.

Now I've lived in America for over three decades—longer than I lived in Ireland. Still, on both sides of the Atlantic, there is a large part of my American life that feels secret. Often, this is my own doing, and this invisibility is made easier by the fact that many folks here auto-associate "immigrant" with "non-white" or "doesn't speak American English." As a Caucasian, long-term immigrant, I often "pass" as American and there are times when I let this happen.

Meanwhile, Ireland now tags us emigrants as "expats," while it tags its in-bound immigrants as . . . well, immigrants.

At least once a week, I have a repeating dream in which I wake up with my heart pounding. In the dream, my American venture has suddenly failed and now, I must repatriate to rural Ireland where, in middle age, I have no country and no money. The dream startles me awake. As I lie there staring at the ceiling fan above my bed, I wonder how many of us immigrants live with this persistent fear that one day, all that we have built and loved in America will disappear. I also wonder what my American neighbors or boss or colleagues would say if I ever divulged the fears, the imperfect and jittery belonging that I lock away in my car as I park it on my neighborhood street or out of the noontime sun in the corporate plaza parking lot.

My Dublin college friends weren't bad people. They simply didn't or couldn't see beyond my clothes or accent to actually know me. Why? Because at twenty or forty or sixty, many of us conduct a lifelong masquerade ball in which we hide our deepest selves.

    This is where literature and storytelling can save us. Our stories have the power to cut through the dinner-party chatter and our quick, facile assumptions. Whether we tell our stories in our native languages or in a blended patois or in our best American or British English, whether they are rendered in song or pictures or dance or writing, stories are our bridge between what we presume to know and what we really should.

FOREWORD

Some days I stand under my shower and belt out Paul Simon's "American Tune:"

> *Many's the time I've been mistaken*
> *And many times confused*
> *Yes, and often felt forsaken*
> *And certainly misused*
> *But I'm all right, I'm all right*
> *I'm just weary to my bones*
> *Still, you don't expect to be*
> *Bright and bon vivant*
> *So far away from home, so far away from home*

My husband and I live in an old, tightly packed New England neighborhood, so who knows what the neighbors think on those open-window mornings when I sing this anthem for my adopted country?

In his 1973 song, Paul Simon depicts an America of intergenerational and existential exile, where we all—native born and immigrants alike—exist in a state of imperfect belonging, during "the age's most uncertain hour." For us long-tenured immigrants, this imperfect belonging now applies to both our native *and* adopted countries.

Often, this sense of existential displacement comes with a peculiar and persistent energy. For me, that energy is part of the attraction, the allure of living in America. Untethered from tradition or native history or family "brand," I can be and remain in perpetual start-up mode.

For years, I have kept this conflicted sense of place to myself—at least in public.

Then, I wrote this collection's title essay and read it aloud at a literary fundraiser. Once published and read, the essay was out and so was I. I had taken a small step to transcend the public persona (Caucasian, middle-class, professional) to give voice to this jittery feeling that often keeps me awake after dark. After "Green Card," the other essays followed.

As I wrote and published each piece, I was acutely aware of the fact I'm among the privileged who have the luxury and legal status and retrospective objectivity to be able to express my own opinions and write down my own story.

Of course, in America or elsewhere, there is no singular or unified "immigrant experience."

However, the more we give voice to the individual experience, the more we celebrate the diversity and nuances and changing states or inherited memories of immigration, the more we force ourselves to acknowledge our own history and our own, deeper selves.

Every year, on my American landing-day anniversary, I replay that freezing December day when I landed alone in New York at age 24 with a rucksack and $200 cash (borrowed). It was long before Google maps or cell phones or TripAdvisor.

Nowadays, my cautious, middle-aged self slaps my forehead to ask that naïve and petrified younger version of me: "What the heck did you do?"

This essay collection is my attempt to answer that question. I want to try and answer it for myself, for other immigrants *and* for my American-born readers, for all our ill-at-ease and battered souls that Paul Simon wrote and sang about and that, at least one morning per week, I love to sing about in my American shower.

COLOR ME BEAUTIFUL, AMERICA

Our old farmhouse in County Mayo had a big kitchen closet stuffed with American fashions. I recall two Jackie O-style shift dresses—one teal, one scarlet. There was a child's dress in Popsicle orange gingham. Lots of sleeveless blouses in bold prints. Lemon hued pedal pushers. A mackintosh in bright fuchsia, and, on the closet's bottom shelf, a pink satin and tulle debutante's dress that was too full and flouncy for a storage box.

The clothes were gifts from my great-aunt Minnie, who mailed an annual box of hand-me-downs from her home in New York.

Two generations earlier, in 1905, Aunt Minnie had emigrated from that same house and farm, and the records show that she arrived at Ellis Island on May 19. She was 17 and carried ten dollars.

By the 1960s, she was a glamorous Long Island matriarch who could afford to ship her American-born family's castoffs to us, the Irish relatives.

Such home-country remittances or gifts are a long and duty-bound tradition among immigrant groups. But in arch-conservative, 1960s Ireland, there was one big problem with my aunt's generosity: No respectable family in our parish would let a daughter leave the house in yellow pedal pushers.

Still, nothing was as exciting as watching John, our village postman, dismount from his black bicycle to stride across to the kitchen door with the news: There was a foreign box—too big and heavy for his bicycle—waiting for us at the village post office. My two brothers were dispatched across the fields to fetch home the goodies from a set of cousins we knew only from snapshots.

We girls got clothes. Most years, the boys got dog-eared comic books bearing too many exclamation points and baffling storylines.

One year, circa 1969, we girls received a pair of turquoise corduroys with pockets in the front and back—I had never felt or seen anything so plush and exotic, and what was anyone supposed to keep in all those pockets? Now, as everyone knew, slacks—if not the turquoise kind—were just for men and boys. We double checked the gift tag and my aunt's perfect handwriting. Yes, indeed, they were for us. Alas, they, too, were destined for the kitchen storage closet.

Some Saturdays, I got up before sunrise and tiptoed through the sleeping house to switch on the light and unlatch the closet's double doors to play dress up. The colored blouses hit half-way down my thighs, while the red and teal shift dresses fell beyond my ankles. But as I swished around our turf-smoky little kitchen, I was transported to a place where it was sunny enough to go without sleeves or cardigans. I held those turquoise corduroys against myself. Unfettered by my hand-knit sweaters and brown tartan skirts, just how fast and far could an eight-year-old schoolgirl run?

Except for these weekend dress-up games, the only time we foraged through that closet was to strip some of the items for parts. Once, I ripped the giant bow off that debutante's dress to make angel's wings for a school play. Twisted together, the comic books made excellent draft stoppers to stuff around our rear kitchen window. My thrifty and demure mother began to wear her fuchsia mackintosh in the upper farmyard, safe from peering eyes and parish gossips. I can still picture her there, her chic New York coat converted to a kind of surgical scrub to muck out the stable stalls.

One day, when I was nine, we left that house for a much better and bigger abode within walking distance of our family farm. This was also around the time when Aunt Minnie, then over eighty, departed New York for a place called Oregon, where she spent her final years with her only son.

The American deliveries stopped. Ireland joined the European Union. My mother bought me a Marcia-Brady-styled polyester pantsuit in navy blue with red trim. Without heat or maintenance, our ancestral farmhouse caved in upon itself. Two centuries' worth of thatch and rubble collapsed upon and around that closet that had been my own America—a bright, iconic country where, at least back then, an immigrant woman could wear dresses just like those worn by the late President's wife.

AMERICA THE STORY

The Americans said I had courage.

They'd say it while I stood there in my black waitress's apron reciting the daily lunch specials.

"Are you from Ireland?"

"Yes, I am."

"How long have you been over here?"

"Three months." Later, "six months." Then, "nine months." Then, "two years."

"Family or alone? Job or college?"

Mostly, the wife asked these first questions. The husband had his own set of queries: "North or south? Catholic or Protestant? Are your French fries hand cut or frozen?"

Raising my voice over the Irish-American ballads on the pub stereo, I dished up my story.

"Oh, my God!" The woman would say. "That must have taken such courage."

In the eyes of these chino-clad couples *en route* to the family cottage in the Adirondacks, I was a hardy adventurer who strode across airports with nothing between her and the big bad world but a backpack and a *Lonely Planet* Guide.

Often, as I stood there with my pen and order pad, I wondered if that American woman glimpsed herself at my age, if my story evoked her own regrets, her own botched tests of courage. Did she mourn that job or that lover that her small-town mother had talked her out of? Had she spent an adult life, a marriage, wondering about that man whose cologne and touch she can still conjure? A man far sexier but riskier than the paunchy husband inquiring about his lunchtime French fries?

In the end, it was easy to defuse the whole courage thing, to divert this nice couple back to their lunch order. It was extra easy if I laid on the Irish accent: "Oh, now, I don't know would you call it courage or a streak of daftness."

My *Lonely Planet* courage odyssey began on a Friday morning, November 28, 1986, when I boarded a double decker bus for Ballsbridge, a suburb just south of Dublin's City Centre. As I sat upstairs with my top-down view of Merrion Square, I opened my leather satchel for that last, petrified check through all my get-to-America stuff: the Irish passport, my savings deposit book and my appointment letter summoning me to the American Embassy where I hoped to be granted a U.S. visa.

Earlier that same year, U.S. Representative Brian Donnelly, a Massachusetts Democrat, had sponsored an immigrant reform law that provided a first-come-first-served visa lottery program that would become named for Donnelly, its sponsor. Among the reported 10,000 visas issued to residents of thirty-six nationalities, 40%—or 4,161—went to the Irish.

Most of us fleeing 1980s Ireland were either out of work or grossly under employed in a nation where, in some small towns, the unemployment rate hit 20%.

Four years before my November Visa Day, I had graduated from my Dublin college as a primary school teacher—a career choice that was more inherited than chosen and that would, as it turned out, lead me into some dark cul de sacs of the mind and heart. The biggest or most obvious dead-end was the fact that, national unemployment rates aside, the degree qualified me for nothing else except teaching children.

Postgraduation, I had worked for four years in a ramshackle parochial school in the Irish midlands. There, in a little crossroads village on the leeside of the then-northern Irish border, some folks warned me that there were indeed Protestants about—but, as one woman put it, "you always know one of them because of that yellowish tinge to their faces."

The school blackboards were turned green with age, and in my mixed-grade classroom, in an island nation, some of my little students had never seen the ocean (just over an hour away in County Sligo). We had no staff toilet, so my most vivid memory of teaching is not of the school or my career, but of pounding up the stairs to my attic flat, my bladder bursting and counting the seconds until I could finally pee.

Then, one Saturday morning, there came that day when neither my mind nor my heart nor my bladder could do it for another day, much less for the expected lifetime.

On that Dublin-city double decker bus, I was nobody's image of feminine courage. I was too terrified to behold anything larger or scarier than that short bus ride and my upcoming interview and the cold, drizzly morning out the bus window.

But if this big-picture view was scary, the immediate alternative was a hundred times scarier: What if I flunked my Embassy interview and had to stay in my own country? I would be a young woman with no job, no place to live, and just enough money to see me to the upcoming Christmas holiday.

At the American Embassy, my footsteps clack-clack-clacked as I crossed the consulate room with its line of pale desks flanked by giant American flags. I stood behind a white line on the floor, waiting for that American man in the white uniform shirt to look up and beckon me forward.

Back then, we collected and shared American factoids, like how much money you could make just walking people's dogs or mixing strange-sounding cocktails in a Manhattan bar or how Americans were always in a hurry and, therefore, they could and would pay for what they wanted. Another factoid was that all the Americans spoke loudly, whereas I had been told that I spoke way too softly, and if I wanted to seem like the kind of person suited for the land of the free, I'd better get loud and bold.

Right. Well, here I was at last, sitting in the chair across from the American man's desk, and here came the questions whose answers I was ready to shout out like a quiz contestant.

Adequate financial means to travel and live in the United States?

"Yup. Oh, yeah. Absolutely!" My voice seemed to boom in that echoey room.

Secure accommodation?

"All set there. Not a problem."

I thought of the airmail letter in my bag, a promise from my already-emigrated friend who had promised that, if I actually made it to America, I could crash on her couch.

Valid passport?

"All there, sir"

Suddenly, he stopped leafing through my paperwork to give me a what-is-your-problem look. I imagined his next questions: *What are you shouting for? Are you hard of hearing? Some kind of anger issue?*

Good Christ! I was pretty sure the Americans wouldn't want folks with those infirmities, so here was my worst nightmare about to come true: I was going to be Lucifer getting cast out of heaven.

My man returned to the paperwork, his face impassive. Then, without meeting my eyes, he stamped my green passport and handed it back to me.

I whispered, "Thank you."

A month later, the day after Saint Stephen's (Boxing) Day, I landed in JFK Airport with a rucksack, $200 spending money (borrowed), and a set of directions for a Trailways bus upstate.

The rest, as they say, is history.

Nowadays, I'm at a dinner party or some evening fundraiser thing, and someone will ask and I will tell and it gets said again: *That must've taken some courage.*

How to tell these nice people that when the walls close in, when all the doors are slamming shut, we auto-rush toward that last chink of daylight?

So from the waitress days to now, the courage thing has always felt and feels like my private joke. I am that girl who gets crowned beauty queen when, in fact, it's all been a secret Botox job.

STARS AND STRIPES AND DAYS OF OUR LIVES

One morning I found myself standing in a basement room in an American split-level house where two white machines stood against the wall. Next to me stood Deb, my American hostess. I watched her twiddling some nobs. There was an instant rush of water. Then, she opened the door of the second machine to produce a half-moon plastic gadget, from which she peeled off a little skin of fuzzy grey stuff.

And then, when you're done, you can just put your laundry in the dryer. But you gotta clear out the lint trap first. My daughter never does. You gonna be ok down here?

I assured her that I would; that I could figure it all out and then Deb smiled and went upstairs while I stood there listening to my underwear and socks and T-shirts sloshing around in the soapy water. Meanwhile, I was being fast forwarded across the light years from that basement laundry room to our kitchen in Ireland. There, on my mother's Monday wash days, we wheeled the old machine out to connect it to the kitchen sink via a thick gray hose. As that old contraption gyrated and shuddered, it leaked lakes of sudsy grey across the kitchen tiles, which made the post-laundry cleanup as arduous as the job itself.

So in America it seemed that you could get your entire wardrobe and all the household curtains washed and dried in less than two hours. Jeans, T-shirts, panties, even the soft, thick towels upstairs in the bathroom. There was no sufferance, no multiple trips to the clothes line, no muttered prayers for a peep of sunshine or "a few good drying days." So how could you call this "doing laundry" when there was no real doing to be done?

I have no precise dateline for my first laundry morning in America, but it must have preceded those other mornings when I woke in an upstairs guest bedroom and knew, instantly, that I was in upstate New York and not in the old, green places I had just been dreaming of.

It's a safe guess that these mornings coincided with that time when I finally stopped rushing to my bedroom window to check if a new, foot-long icicle had sprouted from the eaves.

That first winter in Upstate New York, I lived with a middle-aged married couple in their split-level house that sat three miles outside of town. For this writing, let's call this couple Don and Deb.

Don had been friends with one of my back-home in-laws who was a professional musician.

Based on this music-industry connection, Don had agreed to pick me up from the airport bus from JFK Airport and to give me his absent, adult son's bedroom in that house where you could let your arms jut out above the duvet because this couple kept the heat on all night long.

Before landing here, I had never met or seen a snapshot of this American couple who would provide my first American welcome mat. And that's another thing that I cringe or puzzle over now: From my airport Trailways bus, I could have driven away with the wrong American man.

With the icicles and the pine trees outside every window, that split-level felt like a giant tree house where the frigid outdoors and the broiling indoors were thermal-sealed from each other.

This American couple, who were no blood relation of my own, had accepted me into their home, while Ronald Reagan, via his Immigration and Naturalization officers, had admitted me to his country. So I would have done all their laundry, danced a jig, sung a ballad, or got on my knees to scrub the kitchen floor if it had assuaged or reduced my immigrant's sense of debt.

In the town three miles away, strangers peered out from beneath a fur-trimmed parka hoods to flash bright smiles at me, a just-landed Irish girl whom they couldn't possibly know or recognize. This insta-smile thing was both startling and comforting, and it seemed to appear with the very first eye contact: Hello (smile). How are you (smile)? Cold out, huh (smile)?

So I began to ventriloquist-mimic all this smiling—not just when I was amused or pleased or listening to a funny story, but when I saw a stranger approach, I set myself a test of beating them to it.

On weekday mornings I lay in bed waiting for Deb's hair dryer to get switched off. Then, after the front door slapped shut and her car tires crunched over the icy driveway, I got up and made coffee in that kitchen with its pink counter tops.

Once a week, I took my coffee mug to the dining room table to write my letters home.

Two decades later, after my parents had both died, my adult siblings were clearing out our family home when they found my first airmail letter and sent it back to me. Now I re-read those pages and cringe at how, as well as an insta-smiler, America had turned me into a compulsive liar.

My letter gives an impression of a constant whirl of wintertime house parties and luncheons full of my new insta-friends.

Now I know that this is what immigrants do, what my uncles and my great aunts and my great uncles must have done. After a week in the factory or in the housemaid's quarters, we don our Sunday best for the studio photo portrait to send back home. Whatever has happened all week, it will remain secret and therma-sealed from our families while, in our transatlantic letters and photos, the new country must be written or rendered as bigger and brighter and better than the old.

Before I closed that first transatlantic letter, I thanked my mother again for her cash loan ($200), and I assured her (again) that I would pay it all back when I found some work.

Compared to her previous letters to my Dublin college, my mother's return mail reminded me of the Christmas-duty letters she had to write to our far-flung and mostly unseen second-generation cousins—the American-born grandchildren of my grandparents' siblings.

The penny didn't drop. Not then. But years later, I would realize and finally admit to the source of this sudden maternal formality: When you leave, you leave. You are gone girl.

Except for the letter writing and my roasting hot showers, those winter days were long and solitary.

The first heavy snow came, which meant I had to catch a ride to town where I spent a third of my mother's money on a pair of winter boots—brown, mannish things with a fur lining and ridged soles. Also, I had to abandon my jean jacket and borrow a parka from the coat hooks behind the front door. Muffled in my coat and boots and hat, I launched a self-guided tour through that corner of upstate New York.

As I walked beneath those steely blue skies, the wind creaked and shush-shushed through the pines trees. Someone was always burning timber in a wood stove.

I stopped to stare at the American flags hanging from a front porch or portico. Then, down a different country road, outside a different house, here came another national flag. Later, down an icier and narrower road, there was another.

Had some nationalist martyr just died? No. Even I knew that a bereavement means lowering the national flag to half mast. Those stars and stripes as house décor gave me the jitters, and in my new furry boots I was ready to run like hell when or if a voice called or a dog lunged from a wood-stacked front porch.

Unlike our own farm back home, there were no stone walls or ditches, no solid and clear borders between one family's holding and that of the neighbor next door. The house flags and the family name plaques told me that Americans are really into branding, and that some households kept a persistent and triumphant sense of both their own family and their own country, their own American-ness.

Back in the empty house, I would open the bread drawer to the right of the kitchen stove, thinking, *today will be the day. Today the white sliced pan inside its plastic wrapper will be hard as a rock and dotted with mold.*

That day never came. The bread was always just as fresh as it had been the day before, or the day or the week before that. Equally, the bologna and salami in the fridge's meat drawer stayed mysteriously bright pink.

I made my sandwich and took it to the beige sectional couch under the front window where I scanned the few jobs in the newspaper classifieds.

In those months before my actual emigration, when I prepared to join the estimated 200,000 of us 1980s Irish who would leave our own country, I coveted and curated and traded all those expatriate stories and factoids about cash 'n carry America.

One already departed friend sent me a photo of herself sitting by a swimming pool in the San Francisco Bay area, where she worked as a live-out nanny for a young family who let her drive their 'extra' Volvo car.

"Note the shades," she had written on the back of the snapshot. Yes, of *course*, I had noted the shades and how much bolder and brighter my old pal looked under the California sunshine.

The stories said that Americans wanted what they wanted when they wanted it, and they had the dosh to pay someone like us to get it all done. It was rumored that Americans outsourced almost everything—even watching their own kids or walking their own dogs. You could make $100 per day for painting someone's dining room. You could mix 'n match with two, three, four jobs all at once.

From afar, America had seemed like an etch-a-sketch country where, as soon as your new boss or life or wife pissed you off, you could simply ditch him or it or her for another. Your surname would ring no bells and nobody would know whether your mother wore a good or a shabby coat to Sunday church.

In Don and Deb's taupe-and-pink living room, I could click a black remote control for all these daytime TV shows, including the tanned TV soap opera stars and the exercise and cooking demos and those programs where a cop flashed his badge or a robber flashed his knife.

In those winter afternoons, I became like one of those shut-in senior citizens whose life contracts to a daily walk and a cheap sandwich and that day's lineup of daytime soap operas.

Those TV dramas muted my own inner drama, the thudding heart and the inner voice that demanded why on earth I had left my own kind and kin to come here.

What would happen to me now? Should I overstay my hosts' welcome to stick it out here in upstate in New York? Or should I use the last of my cash to take a Trailways bus to join some of those Irish acquaintances, the cash-hustling compatriots who had sent us all their bravado stories about 1980s America?

Tempting as it was to leave "Days of Our Lives" for the freewheeling Irish, that would mean losing out on America's most alluring promise: anonymity.

In this behemoth country, people can and do cross state lines to run aground in a new town with a new name and ready to forge a new life. In my little corner of snow-bound New York, all the anxiety, all my botched and re-cast attempts at a grown-up life—they could happen in secrecy now. Here, there was nobody to watch or comment, nobody who could tittle-tattle to those back home.

SAINT PATRICK'S DAY

On March 17, 1987, I experienced my first American Saint Patrick's Day, my first offshore glimpse of my own country, cast and broadcast in psychedelic green. I was a waitress in a restaurant pub in upstate New York. The night before, I telephoned my parents back home to explain that the pub would be too loud and crowded to call on the day itself.

"Why?" My mother asked," What's all the fuss about?"

The "fuss" began the next morning with an 11 a.m. queue outside the pub door. It ended at five a.m. the following day as the last taxi drivers waited for the final revelers to make their way through snow banks dribbled with human vomit.

The intervening hours had been a mosh pit of sweating bodies swaying to the band. All this for Saint Patrick, a holy man from Wales who reputedly banished snakes and Celtic paganism.

The entire episode was a million miles from my childhood experience on Saint Patrick's. Back then, we walked to church in our best-winter coats, sporting our sprigs of freshly pulled shamrocks from the fields. And that homegrown, 1960's version is another million miles from Ireland's current Disney-fied extravaganza which borrows backward from its American counterpart.

The next day, March 18, I soaked my blistered waitress's feet and tallied the day's tips. Over one very long day of pushing through the crowds with plastic cups of beer, I had doubled my weekly salary as a primary school teacher back home. Only three months in my newly adopted country, and I'd already learned that the wearin' o' the green had a real payoff.

And a price.

For the next three decades, I would learn just what that price was (and is) each time some stranger or acquaintance mimics my accent—the "faith 'n begorrah," Barry Fitzgerald version. Or each time someone calls me Colleen, because "that's what all you Irish girls are named." Or each time someone tells me the "seven-course Irish dinner" (a six pack and a potato) joke. Or each time I decline that last drink for the road to a chorus of, "Aw, Jesus, you're Irish. You must drink."

Would these jokesters parrot-mimic any other regional or non-American accent—say, Latina or Chinese or Québecois—back to its speaker? Shame on me, except for a wincing glance, I've only spoken up once—a silence I never maintain when faced with slurs that demean other groups.

My own silence makes me wonder if, over the course of thirty-plus years, I've internalized the message that the Irish in America are supposed to be grand old fun. That we're exempt from the standard politesse that tries to purge insult from our sidewalks, our workplaces and our public discourse. From Hollywood to the Hamptons, from the Saint Patrick morning roasts to the "devil-knows-your-dead" toasts, we Irish have fed this sense of ourselves as the group in America who can take the joke—however demeaning and stereotypical that joke is.

Historically, a series of Punch cartoons ("The Bogtrotters," "The Irish Ogre") in the mid-to-late 1800s portrayed the newly arrived Irish in America as drunk, illiterate and racially inferior. The cartoonists gave us a flat nose, pronounced mouth and lips, low forehead, and an air of brutishness. According to one historian, "Americans in the mid-1800s were just beginning to consider the theory of evolution . . . in the Irishmen, they detected animalistic qualities."

In the 1800s, the Irish were not alone. African Americans (most of whom, were not, of course, willing emigrants or displaced refugees), along with the newly arrived Chinese and Germans, all had their ethnic or national traits misrepresented, exaggerated and mocked.

But today, when our 21st century gift shops and drug stores sport their racks of "Happy Saint Patty's" greeting cards, I'm not convinced that the 1800s Punch cartoons are a thing of the past. As I look at those cards with their palsied-faced "Saint Patty's" drunks and the overflowing beer mugs, I know that I've never seen a Kwanzaa, a Hanukkah or a Chinese New Year card that depicts its annual celebration (and its celebrants) through such buffoonish cartoons.

Last March 17, three-plus decades after that first one in America, I got up and went downstairs to feed my cat. I poured some coffee to take back upstairs to my attic writing room.

Until our New England spring comes and the trees fill in, I work within eye-view of the Merrimack River and Salisbury Point—at the crossroads of this country's maritime and industrial histories.

From my attic window I look up river toward the mill cities of Lawrence and Lowell, to my own laboring past. I look down river to the Atlantic and all of our journeys out and back, west and east across borders and oceans.

My laptop booted up. The Google page on my screen was sporting some extraordinarily lifelike green shamrocks.

"Gosh, yes," I thought. "It's a great day to be Irish."

⋙⟡⋘

GREEN CARD

From the office parking lot the GPS lady tells you to *exit south* even though today you are headed north, to the INS building in Lawrence, Massachusetts. You are going there to renew your green card because this is something you must do every ten years to stay in America.

Each decade is just long enough to forget that you are Alien Registration Number 0000-000-0000.

Now, on this rainy highway, you are also Application Number LIN2212703694, and the GPS lady tells you to stay on the current road.

This makes no sense, but you obey because this is something you have learned in America: Sometimes, you must head south to get north.

The wipers squeak. You turn the radio dial for a radio traffic report.

The rain turns heavier. It's 10:05 a.m. You have allotted twice the required time for this journey, but now, you fear that you might be late.

The U.S. Immigration and Naturalization Service doesn't *like* or tolerate late. You know this from the letter that sits in your briefcase—letter I-797C—where it says in block capital letters: "If you fail to appear as scheduled, your application will be considered abandoned and denied."

Even worse than being late would be a fender bender that sends your passport and your Letter I-797C skittering across three lanes of highway. You would become illegal, though your arms, your legs, your speeding frantic thoughts, your sometimes broken heart—none of these feels illegal and they never can or will.

At work, the Finance Department would have to create a new budget line item: "Immigration Fines." At home, your husband would have to pay the mortgage while Harry the cat would mewl around the house for his deported Mommy.

You force yourself to shush those fears. You study your fellow highway drivers—their faces and their phone calls and their frowns. Honestly, there are days when it seems that America is just a very large country set in motion, a 24/7 drive time on looping auto-replay.

You crank the wipers and peer past the next car to check for an exit, a short cut that will take you west instead of south, even though west is not where you're headed either.

It's 10:30 a.m. You sneak along the shoulder while the GPS lady screams about a U-turn as you pass the Dunkin' Donuts and the Richdales and the traffic light up ahead turns red.

The GPS woman says she's *recalculating* as you sit there calculating how long before the light changes. The light turns green and you rush on because it's better to be going someplace than going no place at all.

That day, the day you left, you wanted to tell your weeping mother this. *It's better to be going someplace than no place at all.*

In Lawrence, Massachusetts, you check the streetside parking signs because you don't want your car to get towed to some expensive place where they'll rip you off and they will not care. You check your brief case and your wallet and bring an umbrella. On the way to the INS office you pass a brown building, "Immigrant City Archives." Then, even though it could make you late, you stop on the rainy footpath to pay your respects to this building, to this city where once, the mill girls from Québec and Poland and Ireland worked the riverfront textile mills, and some of those girls had a life expectancy just longer than today's college graduates.

At the Lawrence INS building the security men scan your bag and your coat and your pockets. It's all been done before and each time reminds you of all the other times.

There was the woman in Albany, New York, who lunged across her desk to demand how many children you were planning on smuggling in.

There was that border-town woman in Vermont who made you take another unpaid day off work to drive through a frozen countryside because she swore your Irish Gaelic name was a typo or a ruse.

There was that last time in Rhode Island, where a young man's creaking office chair beat a rhythm with his pissed-off sighs.

But that last one was ten years ago now, and so much can happen in ten years. There have been flights and funerals. There have been tears and parties, arrivals and departures.

You're at the immigration desk. This is the correct room and *correct* desk because you have double checked the signs. You pull yourself up tall because this is another thing you have learned in America: Fake it 'till you make it.

You hand the woman your paperwork. In Spanish-accented English, she hands you a clipboard with more paperwork. She flashes a smile and you want to hug her because here's one of them who doesn't treat you like a beggar or a crook. You think that maybe she has been with you in that car, on that highway, counting time and miles.

At the new biometric machine, she starts with your thumb. *Roll slowly from left to right.* You are reminded of an infant in its crib, and even though this woman works for the federal government, you wonder how many times someone has called her a spic.

"Pressing too hard?" She asks, and you want to pat her hand, to assure her that it's not just girls like her. That you've been called a mick, only in your case, it was said in jest—oh, yes, so much back-slapping jest. That at cocktail parties or holiday dinners they have ranted on about immigrants while they passed you the cranberry relish. You cited U.S. labor statistics, and they said, "Oh, gosh, we didn't mean you. I'm mean, you're . . ."

You think you could tell this woman an old, old story, and that she would not rush you through or twirl her hand to fast forward you to the story's bottom-line point. Instead, you think that she would nod along and wait and listen.

Once upon a time, you would begin. *Once upon a time, when I first moved to this country, I washed dishes in a restaurant where the chefs screamed and cursed and the waitresses clanked dirty platters into plastic buckets.*

This was a long time ago, in a sub-zero winter that froze the snot in my nostrils, in a place where there were so many choices of prime rib and pastrami and ravioli that, just when I got caught up, the dishes started piling up again.

"Next finger," the INS woman says. You wonder if that smile says: *Debo corregir las suposiciones de esta chica blanca.*

Oh, mi amiga, your story is so yesterday.

Sure, we washed dishes and picked artichokes because, back then, nobody wanted plastic buckets of filthy restaurant dishes, just like nobody wanted dirty hotel rooms or entire shops without fresh, California produce. So the INS men looked the other way.

But listen, have you really learned so little about America? We immigrants are not a tribal force. These days, when the deporters search and the ICE men cometh, it's always for my people, mi amiga, not yours.

STRANGERS WHEN WE MEET

I watched the woman cross at the traffic lights and start walking up my side of the street. She disappeared among strolling tourists, but then, there she was again. My hackles rose in recognition, and I recalled something Maya Angelou once said: "I've learned that people will forget what you said, people will forget what you did, but people will never forget how you made them feel." Eight years after my first and only encounter with that woman, I remembered in an instant how she made me feel.

We met at an out-of-state conference and retreat. The first day there, I played hooky from the late afternoon sessions to hang out on the conference center porch. It turned out that lots of us had the same idea, so by five o'clock, the rocking chairs were full and the ocean-front porch loud with laughter.

Some veteran attendees produced illicit bottles of wine (the conference center had a nudge-wink no-alcohol policy), and we passed around plastic cups. One of my porch mates turned to me suddenly and said, "Wait! Didn't you say you live in the Boston area? I just met someone else from there. Let me introduce you."

And there she was: A petite woman with fine, pretty features.

Once introduced, we exchanged small talk.

"It sounds like you're from Ireland?" she asked.

"Yes."

"When I was a child, we had a maid from Ireland. She lived up in our attic."

"Oh."

"Good enough worker, but only when she felt like it." (By now, the woman who had introduced us, embarrassed, had tiptoed away.)

"So are you enjoying the conference?" I asked.

"I can't remember her name now, the Irish girl." A dismissive hand flap.

"Brigid or something."

"What sessions have you tak—"

"—My mother didn't like her, that maid." Then, with a sniff: "When did *you* come?"

"Friday night. It was easier to just driv—"

"—No, I mean to this country. Do you *work*?"

Ah. The penny dropped. Here we were, a pair of women at the same summertime conference, but she had retrofitted me in a black dress and a white frilly maid's cap. For this woman, our shared New England history wasn't one.

I am not proud to admit this, but for the next three days, I looked across that porch and those conference rooms where I grouped her with all of those women, past and present, and in all corners of the world, who blithely let other women fetch and carry and clean and nanny without ever wondering what that servant woman's experience is actually like. In their worlds, this is the inherited and immutable order of things that neither history nor fortune nor happenstance can or should reverse or change.

Now, eight years on, less than a hundred feet of city sidewalk stretched between us. Her hair had grayed (mine, too), and she was even more petite than I remembered.

We were almost shoulder to shoulder, close enough for me to stop and reacquaint. Close enough for her to remember and be mortified. Close enough to give us both a second chance.

Our eyes met. She looked puzzled, then annoyed at this stranger staring at her in the street.

We both rushed on.

Once, I read a veterinarian study in which animal-behaviorists placed thirty randomly selected cats in a room. Some cats instantly clawed and hissed at each other. Others instantly bonded or at least sniffed each other out. There had been no predictors or patterns for which felines would fight and which would bond.

Since that sidewalk afternoon with that woman from my past, I've been wondering just how this works for humans, too. What is it that auto repels us from or aligns us with each other? Is it some secret language between our souls? Or, à la Maya Angelou, is it those careless gestures or words that, unknown to us, wound or diminish the other person so that, years later, this diminishment becomes our dominant memory of the encounter? Or is it our stubborn divisions of social class or race or ethnicity? Are some of us permanently separated by our dueling histories and stories?

Sometimes, I've tried to rewrite our story and our two New England afternoons. Sad to say, I have failed to come up with a kinder version—one that reduces or mitigates what each of us women have lost.

If it's all or mostly down to history, then I think it's not just our family narratives or chronologies that set us apart or at odds.

No. It's how we permanently typecast others in *our* version of *their* history.

FOR ALL THAT'S LOST AND GONE

This story happened during cherry blossom season, a blue-sky afternoon when New England is dappled in sun and hope.

Nine months earlier, before the brutal American winter, I had turned forty. Actually, that birthday has little or nothing to do with this story. Except that, nowadays they say that forty is the new thirty, and, therefore, it's no excuse for middle-age regrets or woes.

Anyway, that evening, I was driving home from work. After our town's highway exit there's a suburban road with a farm market, an assisted living facility, then a city park and a white church.

Next are the old ship merchants' mansions with their ornate cornices and porticos. Then comes the red-brick secondary school with its clock tower and its rooftop weather vane.

A man stood in the school pedestrian crossing, his hand raised like a traffic cop. The street traffic slowed. Then it stopped. It was long after school recess, so what had happened here?

Ah, I thought. *Of course. Tonight is the school prom.*

I should mention that, on this day, this blue-sky day in May, I had been living in America for almost twenty years. I had married an American man.

We would never own one of these ship merchants' mansions, but we had bought a small house on the beach side of town.

In two decades I had mastered most of the American lingo and slang. In the town square, the hipster in the coffee shop no longer asked me to repeat my order. I had learned to talk louder, faster, to drop all those west-of-Ireland expressions that had no place here.

Now, out my car window were all these schoolboys masquerading as men, these pink-skinned girls in gowns, these parents with phone cameras and video recorders.

My 1970s school days were in a small town that had once been home to one of our nation's famine workhouses. In those workhouses, the destitute families slept on bales of straw, and they ate a daily ration of morning porridge and evening potatoes. In 1849, during one brutal week, 96 people died of disease and starvation.

By the 1970s and my own convent school days, the workhouses were, of course, long gone. Our nation's famine had become a set of pages in a history book, a diaspora memory, a round of ballads to be sung.

In the 1970s we joined the European Union, and our small-town had acquired a supermarket and a takeout chip shop and a livestock mart.

Around the corner and up the street from that livestock mart stood our convent school where our nuns and teachers entered and exited like slapstick characters in a black-and-white silent movie.

In the final summer, we sat in brown desk rows to take our Leaving Cert, or school exit exams. Afterward, our Sisters of Mercy hosted a special mass that was followed by tea and tiny triangle sandwiches and plates of vanilla buns. We girls ate our fill, then sat in the front row where we waited to be called to the stage to be presented with our graduation gift of a miniature black bible.

In my school days memories, there are no bright and flouncy words like "prom parade," or "flower corsage" or, "smile for the camera, Darling." In fact, except for the chorused greetings (Good *morning*, Sister), my 1970s school days are without a soundtrack.

My adopted American town has its own pain narratives. But these losses aren't mine. They never will be and, anyway, America is so much better at deleting the paragraphs, at shrugging off the burrs and yokes of history.

By age forty, I had learned that my home and adopted countries had come to exist as separate territories, as mutually invisible headlands across the wide fjord of memory.

On that summer evening, on that blue sky evening in May, a new cluster of teenage couples started to cross the street—another flurry of high heels and yellow and pink chiffon.

Then I spotted that girl, a Julia Roberts look alike in her scarlet dress. In the back, the dress was scooped low, the red fabric stopping just above her coccyx. Her tuxedo-clad boy partner was a modern-day Clark Gable.

Half way across the pedestrian crossing, the red-dress girl dropped her boy's hand to stride ahead. She cast her face into the evening light.

Sitting there in my car, I knew that, at age seventeen or eighteen, this girl already knew her own place in the world. She would assign herself the lead role in her own life.

The Dad-turned-traffic cop waved us on. The car behind me revved and beeped.

But I stayed for one more look at the red dress girl, to mourn for all those missed chances, all that youth that's lost and gone.

SANCTUARY

On Route 95 North you watch the faces in the cars and you wonder how many of these drivers still have parents. You take Exit 56 to drive past the red maples and the farm stand and the roadside pumpkins on display.

While you were overseas in that Irish hospital, while you were walking behind the hearse that ferried your mother's coffin to the village graveyard, New England went and turned itself to bright, high definition Autumn.

Every night you go to bed early because now, even two weeks later, you are still exhausted from the arguments of the cancer ward. Some nights you dream of a woman whose black bones float like flotsam though her molten body.

On your days off work you wander through your old misshapen house. The floors creak. You make coffee. You pour cereal and bring it to the table. You forget the milk. Going back for the milk takes ages because you are trapped in this underwater stasis in which every step takes forever.

After breakfast you head upstairs to shower and dress but you stop at the dining room window to watch your street with its brightly painted federals and Victorians, their window boxes planted with hardy mums.

The side streets lead down to the sea wall and the clam flats where once a man could feed his family with just his clamming fork and a rake.

Some of your neighbors' houses have painted plaques with the original owner's name and his ancient trade: *Nathaniel. Jeremiah. Caleb.*

Chandler. Rope maker. Ship merchant.

These are not the names or trades of your childhood. This is not your history, this Yankee place where the merchants voyaged out to sea and the wives scanned the horizon from their lonely widow's walk.

At your window you are scanning the rooftops, the treetops, and the white clapboard church across the street. You are watching and waiting for something inside you to slip its moorings, to unleash that grief you're supposed to feel.

This watching, this waiting goes on.

On Sunday mornings the cars park along the curb outside your house. Old men hold the passenger door for their wives. You watch them totter down the sidewalk, this Sunday morning pilgrimage to the People's United Methodist Church.

In your mother's and grandmother's country—your *ex*-country—protestants went on fox hunts. In their red coats and tally-ho fox horns, they rampaged across your and your neighbors' swampy farms because, just a generation earlier, they were the colonial or occupying force. They were not these old Methodist women in stout shoes or these Medicaid men in Sunday overcoats.

On Sunday afternoons you and your mother and sister used to drive to a neighboring village where, centuries ago, the Guinness family had a huge lakeside castle and stables of servants and horses and a small stone church.

The Guinness gentry are long dead, and now the castle is a tourist hotel, but the lakeside walks are still open to locals like us.

On those Sunday walks your mother stopped to look at that little stone church that appears in the church-and-holy-water scene in the 1952 movie *The Quiet Man.* Staring across the castle lawns at that little Protestant church with the red door, you mentally replayed that age-old creed: *Step inside one of their churches and you'll be dead within a month.*

For her funeral you wore a black suit to Saint John's Parish church where you knelt with your brothers and sisters in the front pew. The priest sang *Ave Maria,* and he shook incense while you prayed that you would remember the right places to kneel or genuflect.

Winter comes to New England. Down by the sea wall, the tide cracks and creaks in the crevices beneath the ice. The last Canadian geese fly south over Plum Island Point. You are still pacing your widow's walk through the creaking house.

The night dreams are worse now, and you wonder if this is a kind of madness, an infirmity that's here to stay.

One Monday you are stationed inside your window when your mind flickers half awake.

When she answers the church phone, you tell the pastor that you're a writer and a neighbor and that you'd love to rent a place where you could work undistracted. You do not tell her that you must flee your own infirmity; you must quarantine yourself from your own house.

The pastor says she's hardly ever there, and that the United Methodist Church, the church founded for clammers and fishermen and their families, would be happy to have its first writer in residence.

On your days off you stir yourself from the breakfast table and pour a travel mug of coffee.

In the church you set down your laptop bag in an office where the pastor's vestments hang on the back of the door. The writing bag stays unzipped as you sit staring out the long windows at your own footprints through the snow, at a mirrored view of your own house and life.

You unpack a notebook and you begin to hand-write your requiem for a mother and a daughter—for the women you once were, the women you could have been.

One morning you depart the pastor's office to walk across to the actual church. You open the double doors to a sanctuary with a crucifix, the rows of wooden pews before an altar.

All that New England winter you return to sit in this same pew.

The wind creaks in the trees outside the windows and you do not find God.

But you wonder if you're being saved.

HOMECOMING I

I wake to the overhead luggage bins snapping open above my head. My seat neighbor is sitting there with his coat on, his carry-on already propped on his lap as our plane taxis home.

I push up the plastic window blind for my first glimpse of Shannon Airport. All these years and journeys later, I still love this time-travel trick in which a Boston night fast forwards to an Irish morning.

In the early days, I was one of those transatlantic passengers who pre-gathered her coat and carry-ons and then queued in the aisle, impatient for those airplane doors to open. But this morning, my head lolls back and I doze off to sleep again.

"You might want to get off the plane now," my seat neighbor says, and the raised, impatient voice tells me he's been trying to wake me for a while.

In the airport I am listening for all the slip-ups I might make; all the wrong things I might say, like calling the car park a parking lot. The young man at the rental car counter is snappish and assumes that I want an automatic car. He looks askance when I say that a standard economy—just like I booked online—is fine. Of course, he thinks I'm American, so I flatten my 'a' sounds, insert some 'h's' after the 's' sounds because, in this part of the country, they might still belong. Now he turns chatty and patronizing as he inquires how long I'm back home for and what the weather was like "over there." I ask if he's been busy and he rolls his eyes and says, "Ah now, you know yourself."

Outside the air smells damp and, even in this streetlights-and-concrete place, there is a whiff of turf smoke. From the airport I drive the dark, north-bound motorway, the opposite way to all those early morning commuters. The motorway gives way to narrow roads and water-logged fields where the cattle shelter under bare trees. The leaden skies. The roadside church. The woman in her blue mackintosh trotting between a village shop and her house.

It's all a half-remembered dream.

Two hours after my landing, I turn my rental car off the village street toward the wide double gates next to the house. It's just after 9 a.m., Irish time, and still I remember just how to jiggle the gate latch, how to wedge my shoulder under the gate's top rail so it doesn't scrape against the ground as it swings open. In the backyard the collie dog prances and barks—a cue for my father to appear in the kitchen doorway.

He bellows across the frosty morning: "Oh, well, well, well! If it isn't you?"

We hug tightly. The dog barks again. Inside, the house smells of fresh porridge. I plug in the kettle for tea, and he says he'll have another cuppa, just to keep me company. Then, because I'm an American—a Yank—he insists that we take our tea and hot buttered toast to the fireplace living room where, in honor of my visit, there's a fresh turf and wood fire blazing in the grate.

The wall clock tick-tocks. More time travel—only this time I regress to a hundred days like this one in this carpeted room with its net curtains and the front window that looks out at the church across the village street. I hear my accent auto-switch to Irish as I make small talk: the flight over, how the weather was in Boston, what date I'm scheduled to return. He sets his empty tea cup on the mantel.

The silences stretch again. I ask if he has morning chores waiting outside on the farm or in the farmyard.

"Yes," he says, the relief spreading across his features. "As a matter of fact, I was planning on going to see a neighbor." I watch him shuffle to the kitchen, and I brace for the familiar and remembered thwack of the back door.

I bring our dishes out to the sink, then stand at the wide kitchen window. Since her death, he has hooked a line of bird feeders along my mother's clothesline.

Straight ahead is our neighbors' house, a village cottage that the new owners have painted a sherbet pink. Across the patchwork of fields and stone walls, the mountains are a curvy blue line against the winter sky.

I was nine when we moved here from the farm that sits across the fields, just down the hill behind the church. It was December 1971, the year my live-in grandfather died. For that first year the house smelled of its previous occupant, a deceased widow whose family couldn't be bothered to dump or clear out her creaky armchairs and a velvety sitting room couch set.

Back then, I thought the widow's furniture gave our new abode an aristocratic elegance. The whiff of desiccated wood, the new flush toilet that my father installed—these were proof that, in this village of fourteen houses, we had finally moved on and up.

My mother, my grandmother, my great-great ancestors—they were all born less than a mile from here, and most of them in our old, thatch-roof cottage on the farm.

A few months after our 1971 moving day, a part of the cottage roof caved in, and our cattle found shelter in what used to be our kitchen.

Now, standing here in the silent house, I watch this and other memories quiver and shimmy against these kitchen walls. They are old home movies set on mute.

There's my mother digging potatoes in the back garden. There's our Christmas turkey sitting prepped and ready, bulging with bread stuffing on Christmas Eve. There's school girl me in my navy-blue convent uniform. There's college-hippie me. I have hitchhiked cross-country from my Dublin university and now, a kindly truck driver is dropping me off outside the house, opposite the front garden gate. As I descend those metal lorry steps, I know that my mother is watching, mortified from inside the front window.

And there I am on a frosty, after-Christmas morning just like this one, walking out that kitchen door with an American-bound knapsack on my back, choking back fears and tears.

Upstairs, I open each door to an empty bedroom. Slippers under a bed. A book on a night-stand. A cardigan on a chair. These forgotten items are leftovers from my siblings' overnight visits to our widowed father.

I stay longest at my old bedroom. My younger sister and I slept here, in two twin beds with pink nylon bedspreads.

There I am sitting inside that window, a small, blue table strewn with textbooks and notebooks as I study for my state exams. And there's a perfumed, dressed-up me, kneeling in that windowsill to watch every set of car headlights as I wait for a man who had promised to take me dancing.

Waiting. I spent my girlhood daydreaming and willing time to fast forward, to carry me to some future state and place.

I pad across the upstairs landing to my late grandmother's room. On that moving day in 1971, she moved off the farm and her ancestral homestead with us.

Since her death (I was in college), her room has been refurbished with a pink carpet, a new bed. This room was always warmer than the others, so I set my bag on a chair.

In bed I shut my eyes. The sheets and mattress are cold.

Sleep. You must sleep.

My head bristles and echoes with the airport and airplane announcements, the static clash between the American and Irish voices, between what I'm supposed to remember and feel as I lie praying for sleep in my dead grandmother's room.

The red numbers on the bedside clock show 11 a. m.

Sleep. You must sleep.

Lying here, I think how, on each arrival and departure to and from this house, I have shut off parts of myself, boarding them up like old, disused rooms.

WHAT MY FATHER DID ON SAINT PATRICK'S DAY

My favorite photograph of my late father is from a Saint Patrick's Day parade, circa 1988. Now, as an Irish person living in America, and one who despises and avoids this schlockiest of amped-up holidays, this photo preference is a tad puzzling to me.

As the parade floats move through the streets of Galway City, Ireland, there's my father driving his black lorry and, of course, all kitted out in his *Córas Iompar Éireann* (the Irish government transport company) uniform.

In that parade photo, he's smiling (unlike in our other family snapshots) as he turns toward the mystery photographer—presumably a colleague or acquaintance or onlooker who waved or called to him from the footpath.

Back then, my father was about sixty-two years old and on the downslide toward his state retirement pension. Still, there's that boyish grin that says: *Just look at me representing my company in the Saint Patrick's parade.*

A few months after that day, on a transatlantic visit home, I was just packing up for the airport when he presented me with his photo as a bon-voyage gift.

Usually, Daddy left all the gift-buying and greeting cards to my late mother. But once I emigrated to America, on most visits back, he started slipping me little goodbye treasures that were just from him.

"Here," he would say. "You'll need this over yonder."

His gifts were unorthodox, like that day when he came in from his vegetable garden bearing two large heads of cabbage. He nodded toward my airport-bound suitcase and winked. "Sure, they'll never spot these if you wrap them in something."

Once, he presented me with a little wooden peg that he had whittled himself. This homemade spool was wrapped in layers of thick white thread that he had salvaged from the burlap-style bags that came with our farm's livestock feed. *You'll need strong thread over there in America.*

That day when he slipped me his only copy of his parade snapshot, I wondered why I, not his four stay-at-home children, got chosen for this photo that had made him so very proud.

Maybe the transatlantic TV newscasts told him that Saint Patrick's was more of an American than an Irish celebration. Or, like the strong thread and the green cabbage, perhaps he wanted me to have an offshore whiff or taste of home.

Whatever his reasoning, as a woman navigating a series of U.S. workplaces, my father got it right. As it turned out, I needed lots of strong thread.

My father hailed from hearty and hardy farming stock in County Galway.

After their Dublin honeymoon, my father and mother took over her parents' (my maternal grandparents') tiny farm in the neighboring county of Mayo. Soon into their marriage, it was discovered that things were much less arable and sustainable than originally understood. So my father got himself trained and took the test for that lorry-driver's gig and for what would become four decades' of a two-job life (farming and lorry driving).

After the Galway Saint Patrick's parade, I'm almost sure that if someone had invited Dad to join the city mayor and other dignitaries on the outdoor podium for the speeches and jiggy music, he would have refused and inwardly scoffed at all that pomp and ceremony.

Yet, by anyone's measure, my father was a very cultured Irishman. A native and fluent Irish speaker, he could recite long poems in English and Irish Gaelic. He had a lovely tenor voice and a decent song repertoire. A gifted storyteller, he had a quick wit, a fine brain and a colorful turn of phrase.

In a rather recent anthropologist's account of his home or childhood parish, there's an oral history reference to him, the dapper young singleton who played the accordion for the local parlor dances.

Once, I was about ten or eleven years old when the nighttime TV news reported on an IRA (Irish Republican Army) funeral in Belfast or Derry. This was during the heyday of the Northern Irish sectarian violence, so the funeral featured the usual flag-draped casket and the traditional IRA guard of honor marching in their camouflage uniforms and black berets.

"Ach!" My father flapped a hand at the TV screen. "Give half of them fellas a proper job and they'd have no time for making a show of themselves at funerals."

More than symbols or slogans, more than waving flags or chanting for political candidates, I think that Daddy believed that the most patriotic thing you could do was to pay your way and feed your family. And, if one job or fix-it didn't work out, then it was time to move on to Plan B.

Hence: his bon voyage gifts that carried a strong survivalist theme: *You'll need this over yonder in America.*

Two years before his death, when he was already widowed and battling congestive heart failure, Dad's bon voyage gift turned extravagant. Rather than one of his homemade or home-grown presents, he pushed a small white envelope across the dinner table at me. Inside were some crisp new bank notes.

"No," I said, pushing the envelope back toward him. "You should spend your money on yourself, Daddy. Remember all the long days and nights you spent in that lorry earning this money."

Across the table he peered over his reading glasses at me—a sure sign of a quick and loud reprimand.

"What 'long days and nights' are you talking about? I *loved* that job. It was a big long holiday."

So in my Saint Patrick's Day snapshot there's my father driving his lorry in the March 17 parade. True to form, he has signed up to spend our national Irish holiday working.

And smiling.

HOW BOOKS CONVERT US

I remember exactly where I was and what I was doing when I lost my homophobia. It happened in 1983—three decades before my native and adopted countries would both achieve historic and landmark marriage equality victories.

It was a Saturday morning. I was lying in my single bed in a third-floor bedroom in my rented flat over the town butcher shop. A year earlier, at age twenty, I had graduated from college and moved from my Dublin campus to that midland town and my first "real" job as a primary school teacher in a multi-grade classroom in a four-teacher school.

That flat was always freezing, so I snuggled under my duvet to finish my current library book, *The Well of Loneliness*.

The Well is an autobiographical lesbian novel that, upon its 1928 publication in the U.K., got banned on the grounds of its indecent content (it had none).

The novel was eventually released in 1959, but still, I'm baffled as to how a book like that made it into the Fiction stacks of the mildew-y town library down the street from my flat.

Ever since childhood, I had a habit of reading bad. The now quaint-seeming Walter Macken novels were my antidote to the anti-men and -sex screed of my convent secondary school. And, now that I think about it, John McGahern's and Edna O'Brien's early works also delivered in that department.

That morning, I finished my novel and then, I lay there and wept over a fictional love affair that was so sad, so poignant, that it permitted a heterosexual girl like me to empathize with a life that was, in 1980s Ireland, illegal and unspoken. More important, that book had the power to make the alien personal and, by extension, equal.

When you live, as I do, in the first U.S. state to legalize gay marriage, and when you hail from Ireland, the first country to legalize marriage equality by popular (63/38%) vote, it's tempting to be smug now. It would be easy to superimpose a grown-up, enlightened self upon an unenlightened past. So I want to separate fact from memory here and to avoid a revisionist version of that morning in 1983.

No. In this case, I am telling it straight. I lay there cradling my paperback while knowing, deep in my bones, that me and my life were about to change.

Then and since, I've often wondered: How does a mere book convert us from one set of beliefs to its antithesis? Are we writers really that evangelical? Or does the conversion quotient depend not on the writer, but on that symbiosis between the text and the reader?

Exactly three years after that Saturday morning, I emigrated from Ireland to New York where, following a lawsuit, *The Well of Loneliness* had won the right to be published in 1929.

Two months after landing here, I bought a second-hand copy of *The Middleman and Other Stories*, a collection of short fiction by the late, great Indian-born author Bharati Mukherjee. When I finished those stories about southeast Asian expatriates, I wanted to telephone this Calcutta-born woman to personally thank her for teaching a girl from County Mayo that, far from being the provenance of the Irish, immigration is a worldwide condition. More, her writing granted me a much-needed language for the confusion and displacement I was feeling in a new country. Most important, those stories gave me permission to start writing.

While still working a hodgepodge of low-wage jobs, I went back to college to study for a master's degree. In one evening class, a female lecturer gushed over one particular book on our class syllabus—Toni Morrison's *The Bluest Eye*. As white folks, that (white) professor promised, Morrison's novel would be our window into "the American black experience." I'm sure it was. For her. Or for my classmates. But as tragic as Pecola Breedlove's (the main character) life was, Morrison's ornate, curlicue sentences stood between me and the "otherness" that the book was supposed to present.

Then, in 2010, journalist Rebecca Skloot published *The Immortal Life of Henrietta Lacks*, a non-fiction narrative about a black woman who died of cervical cancer in the Negros-only section of Johns Hopkins Hospital in 1951. Unbeknownst to Henrietta or her children, her malignant tumor cells were harvested and cultured to create the first known human cell line for worldwide medical research. Skloot's depiction of Ms. Lacks' girlhood and marriage and death just broke my heart.

Mind you, Mukherjee's and Skloot's books were more enlightenment than all-out conversions. As an Irish woman, I wasn't actively *against* other-nation immigrants. I didn't and don't profess to know what it's like to be non-Caucasian in the USA or anywhere else, but I'm not, I hope, a xenophobe or a racist. And if I'm not, how much of this can I credit to these and all the authors who had the power to change how one small-country girl came to see the bigger world?

Still, I have my blind-spot prejudices, and one is the American military. For years I have blamed our slashed arts education budgets, our unequal healthcare access and a boatload of other national problems on America's inflated national defense budget. In the absence of a World War II-styled conscription, doesn't every military man and woman willingly sign up for his or her government-paid job and that job's inherent risks? So how, I reasoned, can you throw a national and nationalistic pity party?

Then, I read Joydeep Roy-Bhattacharya's *The Watch*, a huge and haunting novel about a group of soldiers in an isolated military base in Kandahar. In *The Watch*, the plight of the civilian Afghan woman with no family and no legs (she lost both when her mountainside village got American bombed) is no less or no more heartbreaking than the plight of the young soldiers trying to hold it together amid the chaos and trauma of war. This book, too, made me cry.

The U.S. defense budget still ticks me off. But, just like the *Well of Loneliness*, the exquisiteness of Roy-Bhattacharya's writing let me transcend the governmental for the personal. Now I see a service man or woman—from any country—sitting in an airport departure lounge and I worry, á la Tim O'Brien, about the things that soldier carries.

Walk through any urban or suburban neighborhood. It's clear that we often choose or default into ghetto-ization, in which we stick with our own kind. From Manhattan to Melbourne to Mullingar, how many of us go entire seasons without sharing a drink with folks who look, act, speak, worship or love differently from ourselves?

Until we do, we must have books.

IRELAND HAS LEARNED TO SPEAK ABOUT THE LOSS OF EMIGRATION

Once, on a transatlantic flight, I was sitting behind two women, both immigrants and both, like me, on the return journey from a visit back home to Ireland. Amid muffled sobs, the younger woman confessed to her friend how homesick she felt in America.

This happened over twenty years ago, and the whole thing made me squirmy because nobody wants to eavesdrop on someone else's heartache. But then, airplane coach class is not built for privacy.

Let's time travel forward to the year 2030 when our scholars and documentarians may create nouveau historical accounts of Ireland's last two emigration waves: our pre-Celtic Tiger 1980s days and the post-millennial recession-era "brain drain." Doubtless, these retrospective and quantitative reports will tally up the totals and cite the demographics: the who, the where and the why. Who were these late twentieth and early twenty-first century emigrés? Did we hail from the country or the city? Unskilled or highly trained? More women than men? What distinguished these last two waves of emigration from their previous (1950s and 19th-century) counterparts?

The profiles and statistics won't begin to capture the diversity of stories and joy and tears. One person's economic displacement is another's once-in-a-lifetime opportunity. One person's homesick is another's escape from a bad romance or a toxic family. If there's one thing I've learned from living away, among all-nation immigrants, we might auto-cite the default reason (economics), but there's nearly always a secondary driver, always another reason for leaving.

Of course, I'm confining my supposition here to immigrants only—not asylum seekers and not refugees, who don't get to choose whether to stay or go.

In the case of refugees, the United Nations High Commissioner for Refugees determines which country they are placed in. Meanwhile, asylum seekers to the U.S. must prove they have a credible fear of facing persecution or torture in their home countries.

If the historians conduct or complete a comparison between Ireland's 1980s and post-millennial mass migrations, I wonder if they will reference how the newer group of emigrés left a country that had, finally, learned to speak emotion.

The Irish-language poet *Máirtín O Direáin* once penned that image of Irish parents trying to hold or behold their exiled children with or within the net or rope of memory. More recently, in one New York interview, Irish and National Book Award author Colum McCann called emigration a "form of wounding oneself."

McCann is correct. Even in the happiest and most-self-determined setups, emigration involves some degree of real and lingering loss. But until this decade, few of us Irish had the license to feel, and the language to speak, that loss.

Instead, we left it to the rhyming or Vaudevillian balladeers (*My heart is in lovely Erin, Come back again to me Mavourneen*) or to the poets or the movie makers.

Indulge me in a brief "back-in-my-day" tangent. During the 1980s migration—and its 1950s, 1920s and 1800s precedents—there were few or no TV news segments of teary airport departures or reunions, no clips of smiley Irish families in matching Santa hats waving "Welcome Home" signs in Christmas-decorated airports. We would have called that "making a holy show." But from where I sit now, these Hallmark-y gestures are a happy and rather enviable sign of a healthy change and country.

Don't get me wrong: The heartbreak was always there, but the tears were bashful and reluctant. If we allowed ourselves to feel the loss at all, it was a sublimated, stiff-upper-lip affair. Or when or if they flowed, our tears were mired in beer or shame or family blame.

In the popular 2015 movie *Brooklyn*—based on the same-titled novel by Colm Tóibín—Mrs. "Nettles" Kelly, the snooty town shopkeeper, laments: "Mothers are always left behind in this country."

For my money, "Nettles" could have added that, for every Irish mother left weeping on the quayside, there's a naïve child setting out alone for a new city or country. Once landed, that kid will go shopping for a loaf of bread on a new street in a new shop where, even if the shopkeeper or baker speaks a little of that newcomer's language, nobody will know his first or family name.

For me, the most resonant and accurate part of "Brooklyn," is the Hollywood depiction of how, once Eilís Lacey (the daughter) steps aboard that ship, there are two separate and mutually invisible narratives—the tale of Eilís in Brooklyn and that of her widowed mother and stay-at-home sister back in Enniscorthy. Between those stories is an emotional firewall that blocks all knowledge of the other's experience and, by extension, each other's respective wounds and losses.

Is Ireland's current, emotionally evolved state the payout for forty-five years' worth of child-centered school curricula? Those child-abuse years, those decades of widely sanctioned corporal punishments, are they finally deleting themselves from our residual and collective memories? Or, for all its prodigal excesses, did the Celtic Tiger, Ireland's 1997-2007 economic boom, turn us into big old softies?

Whatever it is, I for one am delighted that nowadays (and I realize that this is a very broad generalization), if our emigrants or their left-behind families are homesick or lonely or depressed, we have the guts and the vocabulary to come out and say so. Emotionally, we seem to have grown up and got real.

In the years since my airplane eavesdrop, I've often thought about that young woman and wondered if, as her confidante assured her, she eventually settled into her new life and country. Or, if not, I hope she got to move back or away to a happier place.

Also, I'm willing to bet that she bottled up those tears until Shannon's departure doors had slid shut behind her and our airplane had cleared the west coast of County Clare.

KEEP CALM AND CARRY ON BEING AMERICAN (BUT DO WE REMEMBER HOW)?

One summer night in 1987, an American man invited me to accompany him to a country music concert.

I had just emigrated here from my native Ireland, and that huge concert pavilion was my first safari into big and bright Americana.

I may be fusing memory with nostalgia here, but that night, I remember feasting on those sights and traits and voices that would become my justification for packing a bag and leaving my family to move here.

The concert site was prairies away from cowboy-country; yet, most of our fellow concert goers arrived in full regalia. I saw lots of John Wayne Stetsons and red kerchiefs and fringed jackets and pointy cowboy boots—the things that, back then, I tagged as "real American."

Add to these the all-American smiley-ness—that party sense of quick friendship, of shared bonhomie among strangers. Also, before and after that night, it was a very safe bet that, had I been hungry or thirsty or suddenly fainted, at least 80% of those folks would have played Good Samaritan to come to my aide.

That night, I would never have guessed that, three decades' later, I would still be here. Neither could I have predicted that in 2015, I would find myself at another summertime concert at another outdoor pavilion—this time with my American husband.

Three decades have wrought lots of changes and lots of expatriate lessons. The first and best lesson: The minute you think you've pegged America— this huge, polyglot country where many people's grandparents were born in *another* country—you are already wrong. Believe me when I tell you that it's impossible to say what makes Americans American.

However, at a more recent summer concert on Boston's waterfront, I would need to have been drunk or distracted not to have noticed that America has, to quote from W. B. Yeats, "changed utterly." We have all grown cautious. We have learned to keep our mouths shut—at least in public. We have given new and sinister meanings to heretofore ordinary sights and phrases.

"I'm afraid I have to search your backpack, Ma'am" said the concert ticket checker. Translate: *You may be a woman with a grudge and gun, and we cannot take that risk.*

I'm not a jittery or fanciful person, but was I the only concert goer who watched the planes ascend from Boston's Logan Airport and recalled a different blue-sky day and a different, deadly set of airplanes?

Nine. Eleven. Remember when these were just two odd numbers?

America's sanguine, pursuit-of-happiness streak? Sure, in that concession area, there were still some quick smiles and nods between strangers, but nowadays, our smiles have turned tetchy and tentative. There were a few red 'kerchiefs, cowboy boots and the occasional straw and faux Stetson. But the dress up party is muted, too. And here's my big question: What would have happened if I had been hungry or thirsty or suddenly fainted?

For all of this country's flaws, for all our selfie-obsessed selfishness, for all our fears of getting sued, not thanked, for helping a stranger, I believe that America's good-Samaritan factor overrides its fear factor. Or does it? Do I so want this to be true that I make myself believe it?

In the crowd, I spotted a few "Boston Strong" T-shirts. Five years ago, this would have been someone's misprint (Oops! No verb!). But now we Bostonians see this slogan and instantly think: "marathon bombing."

Then there was that guy in the next concert row wearing his National Rifle Association-issue T-shirt that, in large reverse-print letters, told us all to "Keep Calm and Carry Guns."

At intermission, I wanted to go tap that guy on the shoulder to remind him that, in a country that now leads the world in mass shootings, where the reported number of guns exceeds the number of actual people, it's bloody hard to "keep calm." I also wanted to tell him how, First Amendment rights aside, his gag T-shirt is Exhibit A in our crass irreverence for our dead—for those who are no longer with us, or whose families have been shattered by our lax and profit-driven gun laws.

I didn't. I was too petrified. Instead, I checked and re-checked the exit signs and said a silent prayer for all the dead and bereaved.

MOURNING OUR SLAUGHTERED AND DEAD

On September 12, 2001, one of my siblings told me, nearly all the local workplaces in Galway City, Ireland, closed for a day of mourning for those lost in the U.S. terrorist attacks the previous day.

The local workplaces that stayed open were nearly all American. I'm sure their CEOs weren't evil. It simply wasn't on their cultural radar that, on the day after nearly 3,000 people have died, it's never business as usual.

Here's a separate but related anecdote:

Over a decade later, I got hired to teach a one-day workshop at a conference in southern New England. The night before, I checked into my hotel, changed into my conference duds, then plugged in my GPS to find the conference site for a pre-event dinner. Three miles on, here was a roadside sign welcoming me to Newtown—the town where, three months earlier, a young man had shot twenty children and eight adults dead.

Stupid me. Tacky me. Why hadn't I consulted a map or Googled to find a detour? And now, who the heck was I to blithely drive through a place of such loss and sorrow?

Should I pull over to pay my respects? Or would that make me into one of those fetishists who drives across state lines to visit the grave sites of dead strangers—but only those who have achieved media fame?

In the end, I drove on through that pretty little town, but I knew in my gut that I should have turned down that teaching gig.

At dinner, I was seated between a literary agent and a publicist, both of whom loudly discussed their respective clients. The agent was undecided about taking on a memoirist who had written about a family loss.

"Newtown!" The publicist exclaimed. Her voice had the cha-ching ring of a car dealer who was about to close the deal on a Porsche. "Just you wait! When the one-year anniversary of Newtown happens, there'll be a crop of TV appearances and books from people who've lost kids."

The next day, after I had taught my class and driven home to Massachusetts, I looked at my husband across our dinner table and said, "If this is what the writing trade has come to, I will gladly opt out. If I ever try to make money on the backs of dead children, I give you full permission to confiscate my laptop and burn it in a backyard bonfire."

Today, years after Newtown, America leads the developed world in mass shootings.

After these tragedies, we the people lower our flag and engage in a Twitter or Facebook fest of "thoughts and prayers." Then, that day or the next, it's business as usual.

Sure, most of us decry our country's lax and money-driven gun laws. But even if the powerful were to actually listen and legislate, changing gun laws is a slow-boil process. So by the time real and effective reform would actually get done, based on our current rate of mass shootings—and not including domestic or gang-related shootings—prepare to see more carnage.

Laws aside, we must work to address those parts of our American psyche, our country's dangerous brew of best-in-show hubris, entitlement and a kind of rabid version of fame-seeking. In large or small parts, these have contributed to many of our mass shootings—especially those committed by young white males.

We must also admit this ugly truth: There are millions of us who have the stomach to buy one or more deadly weapons with the stated or implied intent to one day pull the trigger.

I say enough with the "thoughts and prayers." Enough with the pictures of candles on our Facebook and Twitter feeds. Enough with our self-spun mythologies about America's bootstrap resilience, our national and faux pride in being able to smile and "move on."

From where I sit, we're not moving on. How can we when we rarely take time to mourn—as in, real, heartfelt, wail-out-loud mourn—for our dead neighbors?

CITIZEN ME

I was getting a coffee in the office lunch room when a colleague joined me.

"Now, you're a voting American citizen, right?" she asked.

I shook my head. "No. I'm a resident. I've a green card."

My colleague and friend is the multi-lingual daughter of Haitian immigrants.

"Why aren't you a citizen?" She wagged a finger. "We need people like you to vote. If you apply now, I bet you could get it all processed in time to vote next November (2016)."

I had no argument with the civic responsibility of voting, but that morning, I doubted that I could apply and get processed in time.

Back in my office, I logged into the USCIS website. The application forms were long and detailed with an application fee of $640 and additional biometric fee of $85. Then there would be a visit to the local USCIS office for that fancy fingerprinting. Then another visit for the interview and oral exam on history and civics.

Plus, in my native or adopted countries, I've never been one to follow the group. I've never been a flag-waving patriot.

As a kid, I got kicked out of Irish dancing class because I couldn't and wouldn't keep up with the three-hand reel. Ditto for team sports. As a teenager, I spent a month in the Galway *Gaeltacht*—a summer language school where all those group activities and nighttime *céilís* made it the longest month of my young life.

Stateside, I've lost count of how many book clubs I've flunked out of. I avoid those schlocky Saint Patrick's Day parades and parties, and listen, don't get me started on Weight Watchers.

Now, as a farmer's daughter, I get that whole thing about building a fence or a wall to say, "This here is my land, and that over there is yours." I also know that, when our neighboring farmer gets flooded, it's our duty to lend her some grazing, to share our own harvest.

Yes. I know. Nations are about a lot more than land grabs or marking our territory. Nationhood is about languages and cultures and religions and laws and history. It's about reclaiming or protecting the national coffers. It's about the national brand.

Then there are those days when a country is just the blurry backdrop for the rest of our lives—the place where we commute and work and eat our evening dinners. I mean, except for the actual words on the license plates up in front of us, isn't a commuter traffic jam largely the same in Montréal or Manhattan or Melbourne?

I have been eligible for citizenship for over two decades now, so why hadn't I applied before this? And, my friend's request aside, why was I researching it that day?

I still haven't figured out the answers to these questions, except to say that in that presidential election year, for women and for immigrants, the stakes were infinitely higher. Also, I'll admit that my trepidation is rooted, somewhere, in that required U.S. Pledge of Allegiance.

I have a bit of an inborn problem with allegiance.

Even as a legal permanent resident, I was an upholder of the U.S. constitution. I don't commit crimes. I believe in the right to free speech. I advocate for the freedom to practice or not practice religion and for the continued and needed separation between church and state. I lobby and donate and pay city and state and federal taxes.

But I bristle at any outfit or organization that wants my unmitigated and publicly stated loyalty, including the right to bear arms. In short, I distrust any setup in which the group ethos supersedes the individual.

I left Ireland amid wretched unemployment and restrictive social policies and during what one Irish politician dubbed as the GUBU era (grotesque, unbelievable, bizarre, and unprecedented). Still, I didn't flee persecution or starvation or war. So as a very willing emigrant, as someone who no longer pays into the Irish tax coffers, what allegiance could or should I claim to Ireland?

Equally, as someone who wasn't born in America, on whom some of the cultural references are still lost or baffling, what allegiance do I feel to my adopted country?

For any of us, if it came to an actual showdown, isn't our primary allegiance to ourselves and to those who love or need us? And, despite my friend's kind assurance (we need people like you), both of my countries would get along just fine without me.

Luckily, Ireland allows us to carry dual citizenship, so I held my breath and decided to download and complete those citizenship forms.

As it turned out, I was part of a trend. From Jan. 1 to March 31, 2016, nearly 8,000 individuals applied for citizenship in Massachusetts—a 30 percent increase from the previous quarter. Meanwhile, for that same period, the United States saw a 34 percent increase in citizenship applications nationwide.

Was it a surge in gratitude or patriotism that fueled the 2015 to 2016 spike in citizenship applications? A funny thing happened on the way to the naturalization ceremony. While we immigrants were paying the fees and studying for the test, Google was reporting a concurrent spike in searches on how to legally move from the United States to Canada.

Despite the citizenship application spike, the entire federal process was fast and pleasant—including the notification for the final ceremony in the post-industrial river city of Lowell, Massachusetts.

In 1822, a northern Irishman led a troupe of Irish laborers from Boston to Lowell to hand-dig the canals that would power the textile mills and the industrial revolution. They walked the entire twenty-nine miles there. Then, once landed in the city that would become Lowell, these migrant laborers set up an encampment and a Catholic church in an area that is still called "the acre."

On Citizenship Ceremony Day, as I walked down the footpath toward Lowell's historic auditorium, it was easy to spot us immigrants. Rushing along in our native head wraps and hijabs and saris and dresses and suits, we must have looked like a huge and very multicultural klatch of wedding guests. Still, despite our bright plumage and eager faces, I had to wonder: How many of us have been driven here by fear?

Almost eight hundred of us, from ninety-four countries, filed into that auditorium. Toddlers clutched their parents' hands. Babies slept in their buggies. In my assigned row, we did our best to pronounce each other's names. We chatted and laughed and we watched each other's stuff during quick toilet breaks.

On stage, two little girls in frilly dresses led the national anthem while their father, like me, waited to become a citizen.

I joined my voice to that large, multi-accented chorus to say the Pledge of Allegiance. Then, I looked behind me at that packed auditorium.

Here were almost 800 stories of panicked or planned departures, of scared or grateful arrivals. Here were people who had taken a gamble—some with their own and their children's lives.

Now or in the past, most of us had worked those low-wage, back-breaking jobs that challenge our human dignity and scar our flesh.

And I promise you this: Beneath our suits and dresses and head dresses, we still bore some of those scars.

Now, wherever we had come from, however far away our siblings or cousins were, here we all were, naturalized and ready to join the American voting populace.

A year after my naturalization, an American-born friend asked if I had buyer's remorse.

I don't. But I do have regrets—not on my own behalf, but for the circumstances that made me print up that "Guide to Naturalization" and pay the fee and study for the test with such urgency.

In my early days here, I thought that the process of becoming a full-blown American would approximate the process of courtship and marriage. We start with a flirtation, then friendship, then a date, then turn exclusive, then cohabit or get engaged.

Along the way, each step, each progression is a very conscious choice, fueled by our own joy and heartfelt loyalty.

Now I see that it was naïve of me to believe that. It was Pollyanna-ish to assume or hope that, when the big citizenship day arrived, when I would publicly swear my allegiance to my adopted country, it would be for love, not fear.

THE WHITE, ENGLISH-SPEAKING IMMIGRANT'S LESSER BURDEN

In America, this is what I noticed first: There were many brown and taupe and black people standing behind and ahead of me in the immigration queue at JFK Airport.

Coming from a then-99 percent Caucasian Ireland, I was startled by such racial diversity. But back then—the mid 1980s—I lumped the lot of us into the same color-blind category: immigrants.

I see now just how naive I was. I also see and know that, comparatively speaking and in any country, "immigrant" applies only to those of us who landed here for economic or existential or romantic or family reasons. Unlike refugees or asylum seekers, even the most desperate of us twenty-first-century newcomers had some choice which was not, usually, a life-or-death choice. In other words, most immigrants are not fleeing war or famine or genocide or persecution.

Eighteen months after arriving in America—and 18 months and eight hours after I had promised my weeping mother that I would be home soon—I assured a nice town judge that the marriage vows I was about to exchange with a tall American man were not a scam to stay here.

Ten years on, as my husband and I toasted our wedding anniversary, I still had no long-range plans to be a permanent U.S. immigrant. But by the time we had marked twenty years together, I had conceded in my head and in my heart that I had become—and would remain—one of America's almost 40 million (the number has grown higher since 2008) immigrants—13 percent of the U.S. population.

What a shock, then, to discover that some of my American-born acquaintances never thought of me as an immigrant. Consider the dinner party guest who ranted about free-loading immigrants while passing me the meat platter. In response, I cited history. Did he know, I wondered aloud, that the first U.S. census to collect data on the birth countries of its residents— in 1850—reported 2. 2 million, or 10 percent, of the population as being foreign born. And the flesh-and-blood people behind those numbers? His forebears—and mine.

He dismissed my umbrage. His wife leaped to his defense. "Oh, not you!" they said. "We weren't talking about you!"

Of course they weren't. They were talking about those non- or not-quite-white people who stood next to me, and who have stood there since, in immigration queues at airports all over the country.

During another dinner party diatribe, one guest took me aside to say, "When we talk like that, we don't mean you. I mean, you're . . ." He twirled a hand in the air.

"English speaking? White?" I asked.

Then there was that day when I was trading in my used Honda hatchback.

"He might buy it," the garage man said, nodding across the parking lot at a young man in a blue shirt bearing the garage's name and logo. "Them Brazilian immigrants, they don't care what they drive, so long as they can pay cash."

Despite what has often been tagged as my "brogue," the garage owner assumed that he and I were in cahoots, and that I, like him, pronounced "immigrant" in the third-person, and with condescension.

Or there was that man at a house party who listened to me advocate (yes, I was on my rant pulpit) for immigrant rights or at least, the promised immigration reform that our government cannot seem to move substantially forward. He stood back to take me in, head to toe, from my freckled face to my good leather boots.

"Yeah, right," he said. "Look, sweetheart, you're hardly what anyone would call 'an immigrant.'"

When otherwise thoughtful people turn rabid xenophobe, when they re-write their own family's arrival here and the history of the United States to disparage the latest wave of newcomers seeking better lives—or any life—they may not mean me. I am certain they do not mean to insult me. But they do.

If there's one advantage to our racially-based and fact-mangling immigration debate, it's this: American or foreign born, it has forced us ordinary folks to take a side. Also, it has forced us long-term immigrants to state and stand up for our own personal loyalties. Over and over, I've been told that I've "done well" (a very inexact and mutable status) in America. If I have, I have a duty to do equally well by our newcomers. At minimum, my tenure here or my whiteness are not a moral pass to shut the immigrant door behind me, and, in so doing, to invent my own, fear- or hubris-fueled version of my own and adopted country's history.

On landing day, there was another thing that I didn't know about America. I didn't know that we immigrants carry with us a burden of proof —of our intentions, our worthiness to be here, of our industriousness—as long as that industriousness is not toiling at or taking another's job.

I also didn't know that, as an Irish girl, my burden of proof would be less onerous, less mired in suspicion and accusation, than that borne by my non-white counterparts.

STRANGER IN WINTER

Out my attic window I write in a journal as the winter dawns over the river and the tidal basin. I hear my pen scratch across this page and I think, *I am home now.*

For immigrants, this "home" business is always fragile. In truth, this fragility or this search may be why some of us left—why, all those years ago, we swapped one country for another.

Some mornings I know that when I leave this chair, this page, this window, "home" will be gone again, and this New England place will revert to being just that—a place, a territory where I have washed up, set up, where I make too much noise and take up too much space.

Away from this river is the interstate highway that runs north to Canada and south to Miami.

Yesterday I was one of the drivers on that wet, southbound highway, swishing under the overpasses and past the exit signs, the offices and condo developments, and there, just before Exit 50, a lone alfalfa farm. I was all dressed up and rushing to a meeting.

Oh, America, I thought. *Please tell me how on earth a woman like me comes to be driving here, on this day in winter?*

These hands on the steering wheel. These arms inside my woolen coat sleeves.

Once, in a faraway time and place, those were chubby baby arms reaching for my grandmother's or my mother's embrace. Later, on a farm that smelled of old mud and wet trees, I hooked those arms around a low slung branch, a girl soldier hoisting herself into an apple tree.

In that damp green country there was a village school that reeked of old chalk and our children's fears. Inside that school I held out my right hand to wait for my pencil, my copybook, my school beatings.

Years later, on another winter day in an airport room, I held out that same hand for my stamped passport, for my passage into America that was, back then, a land of strangers.

Nowadays I keep my hands to myself. Nowadays I will not beg or reach for things that may not be worth all the waiting, for people or things that may never deliver.

Here inside this attic window or away on that south-bound highway, I should not be surprised at the differences, the transposition of times and places, the switcheroo between those past winter days and this one.

For centuries our ships have traversed the oceans and the time zones. Our airplanes have ascended from the tundra to land, just one day later, in the tropics. So there is no magic here—unless we count the alfalfa farm and its roadside grain silo and how, even on a highway like that, there are these people who persist, these family homesteads that hold out against time.

The story is not about how I come to sit inside this attic window above an American river. It's not about happenstance or about all those roads I have taken or traveled or refused. The story is not about me rushing along a wet highway. It's not about the slow and secret tick of hours and days and decades and years.

Perhaps there is no story. There are only my American-accented words on a page. There is the holy mystery of mutation, the bio-miracle in which one thing becomes another, in which the foreign turns familiar.

HOMECOMING II

Two weeks ago, I was heading out for my evening walk when a honking sound filled our neighborhood streets. I stopped on the footpath, excited to watch and wait for them, for that first glimpse of the Canada geese flying through the evening sky.

It was Friday. After a hectic week at work, after a New England winter that wouldn't quit, the migrating geese were a very welcome sign of spring.

In three plus decades, I've never grown used to these North American springs. I've never lost my joy at this sudden switch from frozen and fallow winter to sunny and lush springtime.

That Friday evening, the Canada geese and I were headed toward the tidal basin and the salt marshes that sit within eye view of our house. As I walked along the finally snow-less footpaths, I spotted crocuses in my neighbors' gardens, and the wild beach roses and forsythias looked ready to bloom.

Each spring reminds me of that first one in upstate New York. Back then, I assumed that the good weather would end, Irish-style, in grey skies and downpours. So, I rushed out to buy a cheap beach chair and a bottle of factor 30 and called in "sick" to my restaurant gig. Then, after a week of lounging and reading in my rented back garden, I toddled back to work where, I'm sure, my new freckles and sunburn betrayed my workplace lie.

I read somewhere that, year after year, the Canada geese follow the exact same north-south flight path. Along the way, they stop over at the exact same feeding grounds. Also, as they fly in that inverted V formation, the more experienced birds fly at the apex, relying on their wisdom and their in-built homing devices to lead their flock home.

The birds are a lot smarter than me. As an impetuous twenty-four-year-old kid, I left County Mayo to land in New York with no life plan or career path. I didn't know what I would be doing the following month, much less where I was headed or where I would land.

Since landing in the U.S., I have lived in eleven houses and apartments. Some were a stopover, where I stayed for barely a year. Others were for much longer than that. In retrospect, I know none of them felt like home. But then, pre-emigration, neither did any of those places where, as a student or a working singleton, I had lived in Ireland.

Over twenty years ago, my husband and I landed here in Newburyport, thirty-eight miles north of Boston. Our tiny city sits at the mouth of the Merrimack River, a 110-mile waterway that stretches from New Hampshire's ski country to this tidal basin where the river joins the Atlantic.

Further upriver, in the nineteenth century, young girls from Poland, Québec, Ireland, Austria and the farms of New England flocked to the new cities to work in the riverfront textile mills and to live in the factory-owned boarding houses. In January 1912, in response to a wage cut, a group of mainly Polish women cotton weavers walked off the job. Workers in other factories and mills joined them, creating a landmark labor strike of over 25,000 (primarily immigrant) workers. By mid-March, the manufacturers had agreed to meet most of the strikers' demands.

Despite their grueling hours and life-threatening working conditions, "the mill girls" found time to launch and attend literary circles, and they published in their own literary magazine.

Today I feel part of this inter-generational narrative, this worldwide tale about people who book their passage to forge a new life in a new place.

Newburyport is an old maritime town that has preserved and re-purposed most of its old, red-brick buildings. These days, the estate agents cite and peddle this history, while also touting our commutability by train to Boston or by highway to the area's tech and biotech industries. Also, on any weekday, our town's cafés and public library are full of laptop-tapping telecommuters. We've converted two old railroad beds to walking and biking trails. There's an annual literary festival, a documentary film festival, a chamber music festival, a downtown theatre and cinema, and a weekly farmers market.

On that Friday evening, I walked along the seawall where I could almost forget that we've endured another season of turmoil, of political burn and churn. Since our presidential inauguration in January 2017, it feels like we've been forced to watch never-ending and mismatched snippets from *The Simpsons* that someone has randomly spliced together; all the while hoping that we won't notice the mess. Since then, we have witnessed heinous and murderous crimes of hate and home-grown violence, while also witnessing acts of extraordinary heroism and philanthropy and courage.

Here in town, we exist in a real-life echo chamber. Most of us are staunchly left of center, and I've met many of my neighbors—mainly women—at out-of-town protest marches or rallies. On one of those trips, a local psychotherapist told me that, since the presidential inauguration day, her and her colleagues' clinical practices have seen a sudden rise in new or returning patients.

As for me, I keep on walking. If our polarized and power-or-bust political parties are going to make me lose my mind, I might as well also lose weight.

By the time I reached the end of the sea wall, the Canada geese had made it all the way over and across the tidal basin. Now they were distant dots in the pinking sky, and I could no longer hear their honking. Watching them, I said a silent, secular prayer that was half gratitude and half supplication for this place where I've landed now.

ACKNOWLEDGEMENTS

Color Me Beautiful, America: WBUR, NPR Boston's *Cognoscenti*, March 3, 2016.

America the Story: *New Hibernia Review*, Vol. 17, number 4, Winter 2013 and *Numéro Cinq*, Vol. VII, No. 2, February 2016.

I Hate Saint Patrick's Day: *Salon* March 17, 2011 *and Merrimack Valley Magazine,* March 2017.

Green Card: *Amoskeag; The Journal of Southern New Hampshire University,* Vol 29, number 1, Spring 2012 also: *The Drum: A Literary Magazine for Your Ears,* Issue 26 Cited in "Best American Essays 2013."

Strangers When We Meet: WBUR, NPR Boston's *Cognoscenti,* October 24, 2014.

Sanctuary: *Paige Leaves: Essays Inspired by New England* (anthology), 2012 and *The Drum: A Literary Magazine for Your Ears, Issue 35* Nominated for a Pushcart Prize.

Homecoming: *When Women Waken: A Journal of Prose, Poetry and Images by Women,* August 2013.

What My Father Did on Saint Patrick's Day: *LunaLuna.*

Can Books Convert Us: *Books Ireland.*

Ireland Has Learned to Speak About the Loss of Emigration: Generation Emigration, *The Irish Times.*

Keep Calm and Carry on Being American (But Do We Remember How?): *The Manifest-Station.*

Mourning Our Slaughtered and Dead: Cognoscenti, WBUR.

The White, English-Speaking Immigrant's Lesser Burden: WBUR, NPR Boston's *Cognoscenti.*

Stranger in Winter: *Litro Magazine.*

Homecoming II: Generation Emigration, *The Irish Times,* November 2016.

Áine Greaney is the author of two novels, *Dance Lessons* and *The Big House*, a collection of short stories, *The Sheepbreeders Dance*, and an instructional guide, *Writer with a Day Job*. Her essays and articles have appeared in *Creative Nonfiction, NPR/WBUR, The Boston Globe Magazine, Salon, The Drum, New Hibernia Review,* and *Litro Magazine.*

Educated in Dublin, Ireland and Albany, New York, she has been a U.S. resident for thirty-two years and a naturalized U.S. citizen for two—and counting. Greaney lives and works in the Boston area.

IMMIGRATION, CITIZENSHIP & BELONGING

SHIFTING BALANCE SHEETS:
Women's Stories of Naturalized Citizenship & Cultural Attachment

COMPLEX ALLEGIANCES:
Constellations of Immigration, Citizenship & Belonging

Wising Up Press   P.O. Box 2122   Decatur, GA 30031-2122
VISIT OUR BOOKSTORE: www.universaltable.org

OTHER BOOKS FROM WISING UP PRESS

WISING UP PRESS COLLECTIVE

Only Beautiful & Other Stories
Live Your Life & Other Stories
My Name Is Your Name & Other Stories
Kerry Langan

Keys to the Kingdom: Reflections on Music and the Mind
Epiphanies
Kathleen L. Housley

Last Flight Out: Living, Loving & Leaving
Phyllis A. Langton

A Hymn that Meanders
Maria Nazos

Germs of Truth
Visible Signs
The Philosophical Transactions of
Maria van Leeuwenhoek, Antoni's Dochter
Heather Tosteson

WISING UP ANTHOLOGIES

CROSSING CLASS: *The Invisible Wall*
SURPRISED BY JOY
THE KINDNESS OF STRANGERS
SIBLINGS: *Our First Macrocosm*
CREATIVITY & CONSTRAINT
CONNECTED: *What Remains as We All Change?*
DARING TO REPAIR: *What Is It, Who Does It & Why?*
VIEW FROM THE BED, VIEW FROM THE BEDSIDE
DOUBLE LIVES, REINVENTION & THOSE WE LEAVE BEHIND
LOVE AFTER 70
FAMILIES: *The Frontline of Pluralism*

CPSIA information can be obtained
at www.ICGtesting.com
Printed in the USA
FSHW010306150519
58135FS